FAR OUT
FAIRY TALES

raintree

a Capstone company—publishers for children

INTRODUCING...

PLAYER 1:

LITTLE GRUFF,
THE NINJA-GOAT

STATS:
LEVEL: 10
INTELLIGENCE: 2
STRENGTH: 1
AGILITY: 5
LUCK: 2

STRENGTHS:
Quick-hoofed and competitive

WEAKNESSES:
Shiny objects, paying attention

PLAYER 2:

MIDDLE GRUFF,
THE WIZARD-GOAT

STATS:
LEVEL: 11
INTELLIGENCE: 6
STRENGTH: 1
AGILITY: 2
LUCK: 2

STRENGTHS:
Clever and observant

WEAKNESSES:
Bossy

PLAYER 3:

BIG GRUFF,
THE WARRIOR-GOAT

STATS:
LEVEL: 12
INTELLIGENCE: 1
STRENGTH: 6
AGILITY: 3
LUCK: 2

STRENGTHS:
Determined

WEAKNESSES:
Stubborn

FINAL BOSS

STATS:
LEVEL: 💀
INTELLIGENCE: ??
STRENGTH: 99
AGILITY: ??
LUCK: ??

STRENGTHS:
Strength

WEAKNESSES:
??

in...

Raintree is an imprint of Capstone Global Library Limited, a company incorporated in England and Wales having its registered office at 7 Pilgrim Street, London, EC4V 6LB – Registered company number: 6695582

www.raintree.co.uk
myorders@raintree.co.uk

Designed by Hilary Wacholz
Edited by Sean Tulien
Original illustrations © Capstone 2016
Illustrated by Fernando Cano

ISBN 978 1 4747 1028 2 (paperback)
20 19 18 17 16
10 9 8 7 6 5 4 3 2 1

British Library Cataloguing in Publication Data: a full catalogue record for this book is available from the British Library.

Printed and bound in the United Kingdom

FAR OUT FAIRY TALES

SUPER BILLY GOATS GRUFF

A GRAPHIC NOVEL

BY SEAN TULIEN

ILLUSTRATED BY FERNANDO CANO

Once upon a time there were three billy goats who were travelling to the hillside to make themselves fat.

The name of all three goats was "Gruff."

I'm *so* hungry.

I bet I'm hungrier than you are.

No. It is clear that I am the hungriest goat ever.

Of all time.

I bet I will eat more grass than you.

No. I will eat more grass. I will get fat. *Very fat.*

We're almost at the hillside. There will be plenty of grass for all of us to eat, as always.

Big Gruff was not a clever goat.

CHOMP!

Seriously?

He was, in fact, a very silly goat. He would eat just about anything.

MUNCH
MUNCH
MUNCH

So? How was it?

It tasted a bit *funny.* Pretty good, though. I'm still hungry.

SUPER BILLY GOATS GRUFF!
I am huge! Look at my muscles! LOOK AT THIS CLUB IN MY HOOF!
And look at this shield in my OTHER hoof!
Whoa.
Whoa!
WOW! I'm awesome!
I'm standing on two legs! Like a silly human! *Look at me!*
Little Gruff, you are a *ninja!*
Big Gruff, you are a *warrior!*
And I am a *wizard!*

Yikes! A skeleton!

WHIRRS

Anybody home...?

This place does not look like it has food.

WARBLEG

Huh?

Cooooool.

BOOM!

More?!

Heh-heh. Sucker.

Mmf! RMMF!!

GLOM!

GROARRR!

PLOK!

Weirdo.

I CAST POLYMORPH!!

That's much better. What a cute sheep.

Let's be friends!

Um...*no thanks.*

SAD.

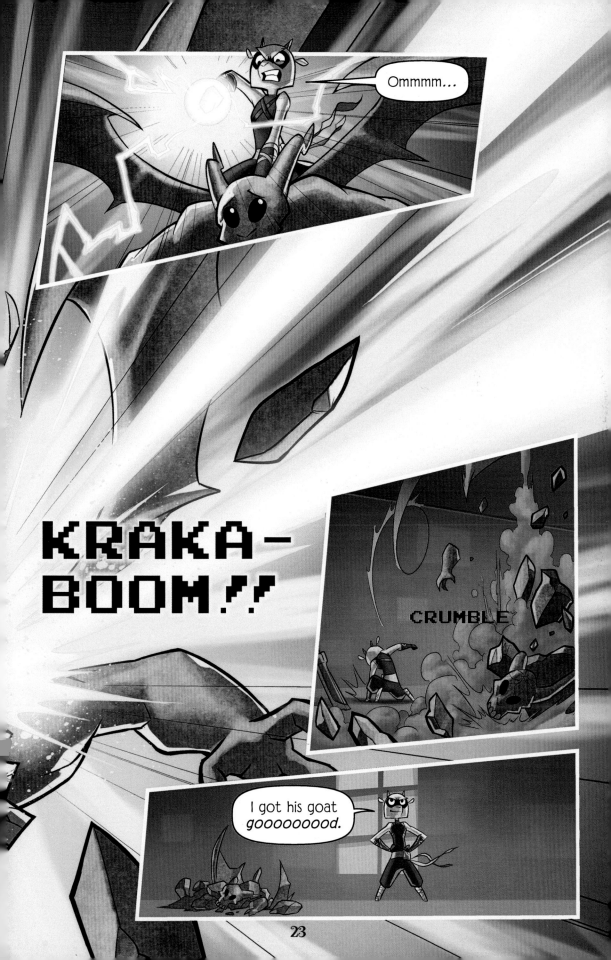

BOSS FIGHT!!

ALL ABOUT THE ORIGINAL TALE!

"Three Billy Goats Gruff" is a Norwegian fairy tale first published between 1841 and 1844. While this version has a video game twist to it, the original version has its own far out elements!

The original story introduces three billy goats of different sizes. They are usually referred to as brothers. Hungry for grass, they decide to travel to the hillside across a river in order to eat and get fatter. However, a fearsome troll lives under the bridge that eats anyone who tries to cross.

The smallest billy goat crosses first. When the troll threatens to gobble him up, the little goat tricks him by saying his older, slightly bigger brother would make a better snack and that the troll should wait for him to cross. The greedy troll allows the little goat to pass in hope of a bigger, better meal.

The middle-sized, slightly larger goat then crosses the bridge. He uses the same trick to get the troll to let him pass, saying that his older, even bigger brother is on his way. It works again.

The third, largest goat is then stopped by the troll, who threatens to gobble him up. But the third goat is so big that he simply kicks the troll off the bridge and into the river! (In some versions of the tale, he bashes the troll to bits with his horns and hooves.)

Now that the bridge is clear, all three goats venture to the hillside, eat their fill of grass and live happily ever after. The troll continues to live under the bridge but he never bothers anyone ever again.

Super Billy Goats Gruff adds its own weird twists to this timeless tale, including enemies the goats fight before the big battle on the bridge with the Final Boss...

A FAR OUT GUIDE TO HILLSIDE CASTLE!

GRIN-SNEER 💀

BOSS

A shadowy sorcerer, Grin-Sneer summons the skele-goats on the top level of Hillside Castle to fight for him. His father, Tanngrisnir, was one of the Norse god Thor's pet goats. He pulled Thor's chariot and was known for his scary, toothy sneer.

MIMIC $

MINION

It has long been said that greed will lead to the downfall of even the greatest adventurers–and the Mimic is living proof. This hungry chest may apear to hold valuable treasure, but its only contents are the bones of careless adventurers.

GOATGOYLE 💀

BOSS

While most gargoyles serve as rain spouts for buildings, the Goatgoyle only pretends to be a statue. This granite guardian perches on top of the roof of the exterior of the castle and serves as the first line of defense against intruders.

FACE-HUGGER ♥

MINION

Some foes are actually friends who just don't understand how to respect personal space. He may mean well, but the Face-Hugger is so needy that he makes it a little bit hard to breathe–literally.

VISUAL QUESTIONS

1 Each of the three goats becomes a different kind of fighter. What strengths and weaknesses does each goat have? Which goat's strengths would you like the most, and why?

2 What is causing the rays of light to extend outwards from the goats' bellies in this panel? How do you know?

3

The beginning and end of this comic book have a different illustration style from the middle of the book. Why do you think the comic book's creators chose to do this? When and why does the art style change?

4

Do you think the Final Boss is still alive? Why or why not? What do you think will happen next in this story?

5

Big Gruff is determined. Little Gruff is quick and curious. Middle Gruff is clever. Which goat is most like you? Write a paragraph about your own personality.

AUTHOR

Sean Tulien is a children's book editor and writer living and working in Minnesota, USA. In his spare time, he likes to read, play video games, eat sushi, exercise outdoors, spend time with his lovely wife, listen to loud music and play with his pet hamster, Buddy.

ILLUSTRATOR

Fernando Cano is an illustrator born in Mexico City, Mexico. He currently resides in Monterrey, Mexico, where he makes a living as an illustrator and colourist. He has done work for Marvel, DC Comics and role-playing games such as Pathfinder from Paizo Publishing. In his spare time, he enjoys hanging out with friends, singing, rowing and drawing!

GLOSSARY

challenge if you challenge someone, you test their ability, skill, or strength

cowards those who are not at all brave or courageous

doomed if someone is doomed, they are certain to fail, suffer or die

gruff rough, coarse or very serious in action or speech

massive very large and heavy

ninja practitioner of the Japanese martial art called ninjutsu. These warriors trained to be stealthy and strike quickly, usually at night.

polymorph magic spell that changes someone into a harmless creature, or an organism with multiple forms

scarcely barely, hardly, or not quite

super extremely good or awesome

vengeance act of doing something to hurt someone because that person did something that hurt you or someone else you care about

victorious having won a victory or having ended in a victory

warrior person who fights in battles and is known for having courage and skill. Warriors often wear armour and use weapons and sometimes shields.

wizard person who is skilled in magic or has magical powers. Wizards can cast spells.

AWESOMELY EVER AFTER.

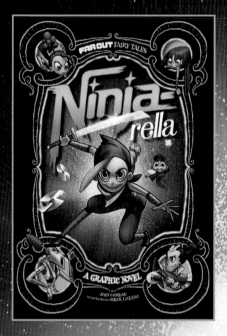

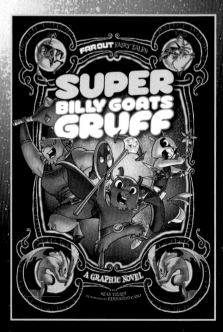

FAR OUT FAIRY TALES